Be Yourself, Like Yourself

Eric Braun

Illustrated by Steve Mark

Library of Congress Cataloging-in-Publication Data
Names: Braun, Eric, 1971- author. | Mark, Steve, illustrator.
Title: Be yourself, like yourself / Eric Braun ; illustrated by Steve Mark.
Description: Minneapolis, MN : Free Spirit Publishing, an imprint of Teacher Created Materials, [2025] | Series: Little laugh & learn series | Audience: Ages 6–9
Identifiers: LCCN 2023050571 (print) | LCCN 2023050572 (ebook) | ISBN 9798885544474 (paperback) | ISBN 9798885544481 (ebook) | ISBN 9798885544498 (epub)
Subjects: LCSH: Self-esteem in children--Juvenile literature. | BISAC: JUVENILE NONFICTION / Social Topics / Self-Esteem & Self-Reliance | JUVENILE NONFICTION / Social Topics / Emotions & Feelings
Classification: LCC BF723.S3 B758 2025 (print) | LCC BF723.S3 (ebook) | DDC 155.4/182--dc23/eng/20240221
LC record available at https://lccn.loc.gov/2023050571
LC ebook record available at https://lccn.loc.gov/2023050572

Edited by Marjorie Lisovskis
Cover and interior design by Courtenay Fletcher
Illustrations by Steve Mark

Printed by: 70548
Printed in: China
PO#: 11570

Free Spirit Publishing
An imprint of Teacher Created Materials
9850 51st Avenue North, Suite 100
Minneapolis, MN 55442
(612) 338-2068
help4kids@freespirit.com
freespirit.com

CONTENTS

BAZILLION FLAVORS

CHAPTER 1

This book is about a big question. Something really important. Even more important than "What's your favorite flavor of ice cream?"

Here it is: **What makes you YOU?**

There are lots of ways to answer this. Part of it is your favorite things, like music, games, sports, movies, and (yep!) ice cream. Part of it is the people in your life. You are someone's child, someone's friend. You might be somebody's sister, or grandson, or cousin.

Your thoughts and feelings play a big part too. So do things like how tall you are or how short your hair is.

Maybe you have a mole on your nose or a dimple on your chin.

Maybe your voice is loud or soft. You look the way you look. You talk the way you talk.

All these things add up to make *you* YOU.

The amazing thing is that there is no other you. You are the only *you*. You matter. You are important, just the way you are.

It's true—you are! We all are. Everyone is important. Everyone matters.

Sometimes you might forget what makes you special. This book can help you remember. It's all about ways to boost your **self-esteem**.

What is self-esteem?

That's what the next chapter is about.

CHAPTER 2

All About Self-Esteem

Do you know someone who seems really confident? Someone who believes in themself so much that they almost **glow**?

It seems like everything is easy for them.

Maybe it's a kid at school who has lots of friends.

Maybe it's someone who runs faster than anyone else.

Maybe it's a kid who gets perfect grades without even trying.

Maybe it's someone who's so confident that they can juggle three balls at a time. While riding a skateboard. Wearing mittens.

You Gotta Look Inside

How do some kids get so confident? Are they just lucky?

The truth is, those kids *might* be confident. Or they might not. You can't really know what they feel inside.

How you feel about yourself inside is called **self-esteem**.

?
#1

If you have positive self-esteem, you mostly feel good about yourself. And that helps you feel confident.

When you have strong self-esteem:

- You believe in yourself.
- You are proud of yourself.
- You know you can try hard things.
- You expect people to like you and accept you.

3rd

What Does Low Self-Esteem Feel Like?

You know that people with positive self-esteem feel good about themselves. What about people who don't feel very good about themselves?

Lots of people feel low self-esteem sometimes. Remember those kids from earlier who seemed so confident?

The boy with lots of friends might worry sometimes that his friends don't really like him.

The athletic girl might wish she was great at writing stories.

The kid with amazing grades might feel like they're only good enough when their work is perfect. But no one can do that *all* the time.

What about you? What if you don't feel very confident some (or a lot) of the time? The good news is you can make your self-esteem stronger. Keep reading to learn how.

CHAPTER 3

Look at You and All You Do

Here's a good way to start building up your self-esteem. Think about all the things you do that you feel good about.

These good things are ingredients in a **recipe for YOU**. What would go on your ingredients list?

What Do You Like to Do?

Think about how you like to spend your time. What do you really enjoy doing? Those activities are the things that make you feel good. Add those ingredients to your list.

Maybe you love to swim. You can float like a frog and dive like a dolphin for hours. If so, put **swimming** on your list.

Or maybe you love learning about things, like how to make paper airplanes or what life was like in ancient Rome. If that's you, add **learning** to your list.

Some kids like telling funny stories and jokes. They might make people laugh in class (even when they're supposed to be quiet). Sound like you? Put **joke-telling** on the list.

Maybe you like cooking or baking. Or maybe you're the person in your home who helps everyone with the devices. Phones, apps, remote controls . . . you figure them out in a flash. You know what to put on your list.

There are lots of other possible ingredients. Things like:

- playing video games
- building with Lego bricks
- singing
- drawing
- storytelling
- doing science experiments
- or something else!

How Do You Show You Care?

Some of the things that make you YOU are not only *about* you. (Was that too many *yous*? Better get *yous* to it.)

Some of your ingredients show up in how you feel and act toward others.

For example:

- Are you kind to people?
- Are you nice to animals?
- Do you help out at home?
- Do you want your friends to be happy?
- Do you care about the environment?

Have you already started that list? If not, do it now! Get a pen or pencil and a piece of paper. Or use a tablet or other device. Give your list a title, like "My Ingredients" or "What Makes Me *Me*."

List things you are good at or enjoy a lot. Also include ways you show you care.

Keep your list, and add to it when you think of new things. These are like superfoods in the recipe of YOU. Yum!

What Did You Do Today?

Here's a trick. It can help you think about you and everything you do. Try to end each day by thinking about at least one thing you did well that day. Or think about one thing you are proud of.

I helped Anita with her math.

I went to the dentist even though I was scared.

I practiced dribbling for 20 minutes.

I learned a new knitting stitch.

I ate my broccoli (even though I didn't want to).

See that? Aren't you proud to be you?

Bonus Tip! If you like, you can start a new list called "I Can" or "What I Feel Proud About."

Look at Who Loves Y-O-U

Self-esteem is how you feel about your SELF. That makes sense—it's in the name! But luckily you're not all by your SELF in life. You **matter** to other people.

Who are the people who love you? Who believe in you? Who treat you well?

These people help build up your self-esteem. Think of these people as your Self-Esteem Team. They are there for YOU.

Who's on Your Self-Esteem Team?

Your Self-Esteem Team is made up of people you trust. Start by thinking about grown-ups in your life who love or support you. This can be parents, stepparents, grandparents, aunts, uncles, or other family adults. It can also be teachers, coaches, religious leaders, counselors, or family friends.

Then think about other kids who are usually on your side. This can include siblings, cousins, and good friends.

Make a list of all those grown-ups and kids who love you, believe in you, or have your back. Give your list a title like "My Self-Esteem Team."

Every person on your list can help build up your self-esteem, just by loving you or caring about you. So keep your list, and look at it when you need a boost.

Your list can grow and change. You might remember to add someone else. Or you might make a new friend. When you do, put them on the list!

Make Memories

Try to think of ways you can spend more time with the people on your list. You might see if you can set up a time to hang with your cousin who taught you how to jump rope. Or ask if you can go with your aunt next time she goes fishing.

Better yet: Ask one of the special adults on your list what they like about you. This is an AWESOME way to build up your self-esteem.

CHAPTER 5

Three Ways to Keep Your Self-Esteem Going Strong

Sometimes you feel down. Your self-esteem might dip.

Maybe something happens that makes you feel bad, like not doing as well as you want on a test. Or accidentally saying something that hurts your best friend's feelings. Or maybe you don't know why—you just feel kind of . . . blue.

Everyone feels blue sometimes. But there are things you can do to feel better. This chapter has three ideas to help you do that.

1. Think Confident Thoughts

You have a lot of power over your feelings. It all starts with how you talk to yourself in your mind. Really! Your own words can help you feel better about yourself.

The way we talk to ourselves in our minds is called **self-talk**. You can use it to tell yourself kind and encouraging things.

I'm getting better!

Every day, think of all the good things you can do and *do* do.

Start with something you like about yourself. (Look at the list of recipe ingredients you started in Chapter 3.) It could be something . . .

✔ you are proud of

- "I'm a good listener to my friends."

- "I know a lot about camping."

- "I studied hard for the quiz."

- "My little sister looks up to me."

✓ you enjoy

- "I love bowling."

Next, add why this is such an important part of YOU.

- "I love bowling. It's a fun thing to do with friends. When I go bowling with Marco, we both laugh a lot, even when we miss!"

2. Be Honest

It's good to remember what you're good at. But that doesn't mean you pretend everything is super-duper great all the time.

Sometimes things don't go as planned. Sometimes you mess up. Sometimes you try and try, but you just aren't quite *there* yet. It happens to everyone.

When it happens to you, you can still think confident thoughts. But be honest with yourself too.

Your confident self-talk about the things you *are* good at is only meaningful if you're also honest about the other stuff. It's also important to be honest

with others. Tell the truth about the things that go right *and* the things that go wrong. Don't exaggerate your accomplishments.

When you are honest with others, they respect you for your honesty. And it feels good to have that respect. More good news for your self-esteem!

3. Take Care of Yourself

Take care of your body.

Eat fruits and veggies and limit snack foods like sweets and fried treats.

Get exercise. Get rest and sleep too.

These are not just things that grown-ups tell you to do. They are all ways you show respect for yourself. They are good for your self-esteem.

Treat yourself like you are important. Because you ARE important!

CHAPTER 6

Six Ways to Bounce Back from Setbacks

Of course, having strong self-esteem doesn't mean you *always* feel good about yourself. Bad times and blue moods happen to everyone. Even famous athletes and movie stars. Even that juggling kid on the skateboard.

Strong self-esteem can help you get through hard times.

When you have strong self-esteem:

- You keep trying when things are hard or don't go well.
- You like and trust yourself even when you make mistakes.
- You accept yourself even when others criticize you.

In other words, you **bounce back** from **setbacks**. This chapter has six ideas to help you do this!

1. Keep Trying When Something Is Hard

Most people don't get things right the first time. Or the second time. Or even the third. So keep on trying, even when something is hard.

But keep in mind that it's **impossible** for anyone to be **perfect**. So don't try! It's good to keep working on something that's important to you, but don't expect to win every game.

Or get 100 on every quiz.

Or make everyone laugh each time you tell a joke.

Or learn something new the first time, every time.

Or . . . well, you get the idea.

2. Learn from Mistakes

Hey, mistakes show you what *doesn't* work—so you can figure out what does!

I think I'm finally getting it!

3. Try Not to Compare Yourself to Others

If you notice yourself doing this, use your self-talk to remind yourself of all the strong, good things about you. You are special and unique!

What matters is what *you* do. If you want to compare, compare yourself to . . . yourself! Look at how you've grown, gotten better, or tried harder.

PHOTO
CONTEST
2nd
PLACE
3rd
PLACE
HONORABLE
MENTION

4. Don't Believe Unkind Words from Others

Has anyone ever been unkind to you? Have people left you out? Maybe someone said mean things about you or your family.

Sometimes, people aren't nice. Boooo!

This can be a real drag on your self-esteem.

You can protect your self-esteem when people are unkind by always remembering what's good about you. What other people do or say does not affect who you really are.

What's important is what you know on the inside. So keep thinking of all the good things about yourself. Those are the things that matter.

Important Note! If someone is being mean to you over and over and won't stop, tell a teacher or another adult. They can help.

5. Get Support

It helps to talk about your setbacks with someone who's on your side. Tell a friend what's going on.

- "Hey, Jojo, can I talk to you about this kid who has been teasing me?"
- "Frankie, do you ever feel like you're not good enough? I wish I was better at reading, and it's really bugging me."
- "I'm having a bad day. Can I tell you about it?"

Your friend can support you or stick up for you. A friend's kindness is like lotion on a burn. Let the healing begin.

Sometimes you need more support. Remember your Self-Esteem Team from Chapter 4? Those trusted people are just right for this. Pick someone you feel comfortable with, and ask if they can talk.

- "Something's bugging me and I'd like to talk about it."
- "Can we talk for a minute?"
- "Can I tell you something?"

The person might have advice. They might share their own stories of hard times. Or they might not have any advice or stories. That's okay. Sometimes you'll feel better just because someone listens and understands.

6. Talk Back to Mean Self-Talk

Sometimes our bad feelings come from a very powerful source: our own heads! Do you ever have a not-so-nice voice in your head? One that blames or criticizes you? Life can be hard enough. You don't need to put yourself down!

Bad singer.
Bad at catching mice.

If your self-talk is mean or harsh, you can talk back.

Tell yourself this:

- "I'm kind. I can be a good friend."
- "I know a lot about taking care of pets."
- "I show up for every practice and work hard. I'm getting better."
- "I made yummy chocolate chip cookies today."

Full ESTEEM Ahead!

What's that? Up ahead?

It's the future!

Future YOU is going to be great. That's because building up your self-esteem doesn't only help you now. It *keeps* helping you. It helps you feel confident to try new things.

Here's something that might surprise you: When you try something, you can feel good about yourself no matter how it turns out.

Maybe you try a new sport: roller-board soccer. And maybe you stink at it.

That is okay! It's great that you tried. Trying is a good thing. Maybe you'll get better with more tries. Or maybe you'll try something else.

That's a cool circle of self-esteem!

Spread the Goodness

There's one more thing you can do to boost your self-esteem:

Spread the good feelings.

You know those people in your life who you trust and love? Let them know how you feel! You can help build up *their* self-esteem by telling them how much they mean to you. How important they are. How unique and special they are.

When you do this, you brighten their day. And you feel good too because you helped someone.

It's fun to do this with you!

Want to know a bonus of thinking about what you like in others? You might notice things they do that YOU want to try!

Of course, the most important part of spreading good feelings is helping boost someone's self-esteem. And when they feel good, they'll probably spread those good feelings around too, just like you're doing. They'll be more likely to do the same for you.

It's another one of those cool circles.

Hey, YOU really are awesome. In fact, you are the only person just like you.

GLOSSARY

affect: (page 58) to make something happen or make someone feel a certain way

boost: (page 5) to help or make stronger

confident: (page 6) the feeling you have when you believe in yourself

criticize: (page 51) talk about another person's faults or mistakes

matter: (page 4) to be important

respect: (page 47) to show that you think someone is important and their feelings matter"

self-esteem: (page 5) how you feel about yourself

self-talk: (page 38) words you say to yourself in your mind

setbacks: (page 51) things that go wrong

support: (page 30) to help and encourage someone; to believe in them

About the Author and Illustrator

Eric Braun is a children's author and editor. He has written dozens of books on many topics, and one of his books was read by an astronaut on the International Space Station for kids on Earth to watch. Eric likes to toss the Frisbee with his sons and go on bike adventures. He lives in Minneapolis.

Steve Mark is a freelance illustrator and a part-time puppeteer. He lives in Minnesota and is the father of three and the husband of one. Steve has illustrated many books for children, including *Ease the Tease!* and *Make a Friend, Be a Friend* from the Little Laugh & Learn® series and all the books in the Laugh & Learn® series for older kids.